Getting Results from your Analyst Relations Strategies

Getting Results from your Analyst Relations Strategies

Louis Columbus

iUniverse, Inc.

New York Lincoln Shanghai

Getting Results from your Analyst Relations Strategies

iUniverse, Inc.

For information address:
iUniverse, Inc.
2021 Pine Lake Road, Suite 100
Lincoln, NE 68512
www.iuniverse.com

ISBN: 0-595-33462-8

Printed in the United States of America

To my wonderful wife, Cheryl and my cherished daughter, Alyssa Hope. You both have made this book possible with your support and love.

Contents

Acknowledgements

At International Data Corporation (IDC) I have thoroughly enjoyed working with Robert Amatruda, a highly capable analyst with an excellent grasp of the storage industry. At Gartner Group, Fara Yale has been incredibly responsive and wonderful to work with, and a great mentor to me. AMR Research was an incredibly powerful learning experience for me as a servant of others with information, and quickly taught me to go beyond just being an analyst to being an analytical thinker. Thank you Tony Friscia for being a CEO with complete honesty, ethics, and the willingness to tell it like it is to your company. Tony, thank you for investing in me for years as I learned how to be an analyst; I am indebted to you.

I have a passion for serving others with information and there are people who helped me manage the pure enthusiasm I had into something of worth for others. Thank you Rod Johnson for the tremendous education and for teaching me how to make and keep commitments. Your tough-but-fair approach to managing taught me much both about being an analyst but also about managing analyst relations. Thanks also to John Hagerty for your guidance and for your patience with me as I learned to write about what AMR clients cared about. Thank you Bruce Richardson for a very entertaining education as well.

Thanks also to Joanie Rufo, Laura Preslan, Kevin Scott, Matt Thompson, and Kris Iyer for the team we were. It was great working with each of you, and thanks for the endless edits of my Alerts, reports and outlooks.

Thank you Michael DiPietro, Patty Donze, and Dan Birnbaum for the guidance and support as I worked in the client research organization of AMR. Each of you provided me with strong insights and guidance and thanks for your always-constant support. Thank you Simon Jacobsen for your outstanding teamwork and support. Your contributions to Cincom and all clients are invaluable.

Finally I want to thank each of the AMR Research clients I had the pleasure to serve as I fulfilled my personal goal of being an industry analyst. Please know that I was always focused on how to make the maximum impact in your businesses, always focused on how I could help you get to your goals, and always looked out for the return on your investment in AMR. Thanks to each of you I grew professionally faster than I ever had before. Thank You.

Introduction

I've been involved with analyst relations, competitive analysis, market research and product planning for a little over two decades, and always wanted to be an industry analyst. After over fifteen years in the high tech industry including positions at Toshiba America, Ingram Micro and Gateway Computer, I finally had the chance to become an industry analyst for AMR Research. If you haven't heard of AMR, it's a research and advisory firm focused on the enterprise software industry.

As an industry analyst I had the responsibility of covering multiple areas of e-commerce. There are dozens of software companies that create, sell and service applications and it was my responsibility to track their product development, satisfaction level their customers have with enterprise software applications, and recommend strategies for increasing the effectiveness of their applications.

The second part of an industry analyst's job is to serve the companies looking to acquire the technologies that are being tracked and reported on. It's more of being a consultative resource than merely a librarian or reports; this second half of an analyst's role takes more industry experience because you have to tell companies what the best possible solution to their problems are, and where in many cases to spend hundreds of thousands, sometimes millions of dollars.

Combining the service of these two customers into a single role is what makes industry analysts influential in their specific areas of coverage. The best analysts have the ability to further distance themselves from vendor favoritism and focus on the most critical needs of the acquirers of software. It's more about learning from the vendor community to serve the users of technology.

From buying research services to in part selling them as an analyst I realized that there are best practices some companies find and employ to their competitive advantage in the market, and there are also myths about analysts being hired guns. The truth is in the middle of those extremes, and the bottom line for any analyst, I learned, was to be critical of the recommendations you make to serve the acquirers of technology.

Why I Decided To Write This Book

After having been an analyst I realized that many of my clients really weren't going about getting the most out of their analyst relations dollars. Either crippled with myths of not being a big enough vendor to "buy off" analysts or being so large that they thought they should be in every deal with a user I was involved in, the need for a book to show both effective strategies and myths that need to be dispelled needed to be written.

This book is for those vendors that are struggling to get results from their analyst relations dollars. And like any investment, there has to be accountability. The days of blindly sending in $30,000, or $50,000 or even $100,000 are over. The shrinking base of analyst firms is a testament to that fact. If you want results from analyst relations, measure them, and realize that only when an analyst firms is held to accountable results will you get your money's worth. That's the message of this book, and the strategies included in it are meant to guide to you that goal.

1

Why Analysts Matter

Truth is the most precious commodity today and needs to guide all your efforts in analyst relations, anything less is self-destructive and a waste of your and the analyst's time. At the heart of why analysts matter is that they are retained by companies acquiring technologies and looking for guidance in which products to buy, services to retain, and direction to take that has many times a direct bearing on which companies get orders and which don't. In the information technologies arena analysts are seen as the arbiters of truth; they can make or break small and large companies alike. Their recommendations can get a small struggling software company into deals that even the world's largest enterprise software companies could not get into. Conversely an analyst relations program that relies more on empty promises and unproven products is a sure way to get another major impediment in a company's way. The bottom line is that analyst relations are a critical activity that deserves its own strategy and even its own function. Analyst Relations ideally needs to be a stand-alone role either within Marketing, Public Relations, or in large companies, directly to the CEO's office.

If you're getting your analyst relations strategy together today be sure to consider these critical issues when organizing where the responsibility for managing analysts will be:

1. **Product management needs to use analysts for competitive and market intelligence.** Be sure to locate analyst relations in the organization so that the product managers and engineers can have frequent access to the expertise you are paying for.

2. **Public Relations is a critical link to Analyst Relations.** Many companies have analyst relations as part of PR, and that works for many smaller companies. It's been my experience that the measures of performance for analyst relations do vary from public relations, and having

that understanding going into how you manage the analyst relations function makes a big difference.

3.   **Try to avoid analyst relations in a vacuum.** One of traps companies fall into with analyst relations is that they tend to silo it, giving total responsibility to a Vice President who is so busy they don't have a chance to really understand the needs deep down in the company. Be sure to get analyst relations out into the working groups of the company. Having a VP owning the area is great; just make sure their staff is actively looking outward to the sales force and channels on the one hand and inwardly to the product marketing and product management teams for their information needs.

4.   **Analyst Relations is part of a services strategy in the strongest vendors.** Every company I worked with as an analyst that got the most out of their subscriptions took the attitude that analysts were of service to the company, and while we had to get briefed on their latest developments, it was in our service to their departments where the value really came from. Work to get that mindset with your analysts. You have to establish that level of trust to get to a scorecard (which is talked about later in this book) and get accountability included in your analyst program spending.

Analyst Relations is a strategic activity that has to be championed inside the company to be taken seriously by anyone outside. With the goal of being as pragmatic and practical as possible, the book is organized into chapters that guide you through the steps of setting an analyst relations strategy, defining realistic expectations, executing against expectations, and eventually turning analysts into advocates for your company. There is no panacea however that any book can tell you for turning an ambivalent or even negative analyst community into analysts ready to sing your praises to potential clients and the media.

Exploring This Book

Think of this book as a roadmap to making analyst relations work for you and your company. It starts with the building of a foundation what you want to accomplish with analyst organizations, adding in what analysts are good and bad at to arrive at a common set of expectations that analysts can deliver for your company. Most companies get nervous about working with analysts as they expect their efforts to backfire and negative press to result, or worse, lost business. This book is meant to get past that negative view of analysts and show you how to build stronger relationships with analysts based on what your company truly excels at.

Chapter 1 begins with an overview of why analysts matter, and included in this chapter is a thorough overview of the multiple roles analysts play and who they impact their company across product, financial, operational, investment, sales, marketing and public relations arenas.

Chapter 2 defines why it's critical for both analysts and analyst relations professionals to be honest with each other. Exploring whether analysts are ethical or not, the most commonly held misconceptions and myths of working with analysts, and how to get analysts engaged for the long-term with your company are all defined here.

Finding ROI in analyst organizations is the focus of Chapter 3. While you really can't ever look at analysts purely as lead generation strategies you can define what your expectations are and measure them for the benefit of both the analyst firm and your company's management. This chapter provides an overview of how to calculate ROI for the analyst relationships you are investing in.

Analyst tours are critical parts of any long-term relations strategy. Chapter 4 defines best and worst practices in managing analyst relations tours, and provide a scenario as an example of how to handle these tours.

The secret weapon of many analyst relations teams is having a great CEO is completely in touch with the needs of customers and knows exactly what's going on in the market. What's most impressive is seeing CEOs who really have a passion for their companies' direction and are at the same time honest and up-front about their company's strengths and weaknesses. Chapter 5 explains why analysts really appreciate it when CEOs show strong ownership of their company's strengths, weaknesses, opportunities and threats. The discussion in this chapter also discusses how CEOs want to see more and more accountability when it comes to analyst spending—and the following chapter of the book centers on that emerging need many companies have to quantify the performance of analyst firms.

Chapter 6, Managing Analyst Relations To A Scorecard, is one of the main messages of this book, which is to focus on delivering quantifiable results from analyst interactions. This chapter provides a glimpse of what an analyst relations scorecard looks like and the key strategies you can undertake to get greater results from your analyst relations investment.

Managing speaking events with analysts, whether it's for a sales meeting or for the launch of a major new product, takes much effort. Chapter 7 details how to work with analysts in coordinating speaking events.

Chapter 8 details how to deal with transitions of analysts. There's more volatility these days in the analyst ranks partially due to re-aligned research agendas and partially due by consolidation in key markets yet the bottom line is that chances are an analyst you work with today could be with a competitor tomorrow. That's something to consider when you are working with analysts today.

Being Different By Assisting Analysts: You Get What You Give

If you're an analyst relations, public relations, investor relations, or even a C-level executive given the task of managing analyst relations for your company start thinking more about analysts being partners than just someone you routinely brief and evangelize products to. Reciprocity is key to making an analyst recognize the value of your company.

1. **Define your goals for the briefing in advance to give the analyst a chance to get prepared.** This is the best approach of all for getting the most out of an analyst briefing. There is a rule of thumb most analyst abide by: no agenda no meeting. Get an agenda out as quickly as possible so the analyst understands what to expect and can prepare.

2. **Send slides, documents and documents well ahead of the meeting.** This is common courtesy, and not sending them in advance says you're either not done with them yet, will be making them on the plane on the way over (lots of analyst briefing slides get done at 30,000 feet or higher!). In all cases the best approach is to get the slides out beforehand.

3. **There are no excuses for being late for a briefing you have asked for.** Be sure to be early, get set up in a conference room if visiting in person, and make sure everything is ready to go. To waste time and show a lack

of concern on this point is to alienate pretty much anyone in a research company.

4. **Never do briefings via cell phone.** It is universally frowned upon and on conference calls the sound of a cell phone in traffic practically makes the rest of the conversation unintelligible. Never do briefings by cell phone. One Gartner analyst actually hung up on a cell phone briefing that became nearly impossible to hear and blamed it on the cell phone losing its signal.

5. **Don't ever rely on Webex or Placeware as your only communications tool for briefings.** Always have two or three different presentation approaches for analysts, as often Webex and Placeware both will be running slow during periods of high Internet traffic. Plan for the unexpected glitch at the analyst organization.

6. **Shut up and listen.** For many companies in high tech and IT, they make their quarterly or at least semi-annual pilgrimage to the industry analysts that track them starts with a series of meetings to define the messaging, core differentiators, product roadmap, and high probability of winning clients in the pipeline. With agendas in mind and Power-Points in hand, companies make their rounds throughout the analyst community making sure to get the majority of the content conveyed in a very short period of time. Be that vendor, manufacturer, or even user of analyst services that stops to listen and actively elicit feedback. That is the greatest differentiator of all.

7. **The less PowerPoint slides the better.** There is nothing an analyst hates more than more PowerPoint slides than minutes in the briefing. Use the time to chat with the analysts about your plans and ask for feedback. The goal is to have the analysts speak more than you do; get them to open up and give you both their opinions. That is what you are paying for.

8. **Don't quote one research firms' findings, statistics or magic quadrants to another.** Nothing will make an analyst organization tune out en masse as the displaying and actively referencing of another analyst organizations' findings. There is a high level of pride inside each company, so respect that and tailor your presentations and discussion materials for the analyst organization you are presenting to at the time. Don't ask for validation of one analyst firm's results from another. Apart from

the fact that this is somewhat rude, one analyst firm doesn't have any insight into the methodologies and approaches used by the other analyst firms to create their forecasts, market projections, or even something as fundamental as their view on the market. Asking Gartner analysts to comment on Forrester numbers is just a waste of time for example, or asking AMR analysts to validate Meta figures is just the same.

9. **The bottom line is that the analyst wants to make a significant impact on your company's strategy, branding, and style of execution.** Analysts really do want to make a solid and lasting contribution to your company; give them a chance. Open up and share the strengths and weaknesses of your company and ask them for honest feedback. Getting to this level of interaction with an analyst means letting them see all the good and the bad, which is a risk but a worthy one if you want to get the most out of your relationship with them.

Never Bait and Switch An Analyst Organization Just For A Briefing

Misleading analyst organizations about your intention to be a client simply to get in front of their analysts for a briefing is one of the quickest paths to being ignored as a company.

Lying to an analyst organizations' sales force about your intentions to sign up drains your credibility, makes you look unprofessional and makes entire research firms even question your viability. If you practice this to get free briefings there is only a matter of time until payback time arrives. Take these recommendations if all you want is a briefing and you have no intention of signing up with the firm:

1. **Make it clear all you want is a briefing.** Many research companies and analyst organizations will take briefings once a year from non-clients to keep updated on what's happening in the market.

2. **Don't quote the analyst from the interaction during the briefing.** While research companies vary on this subject, it's best to not use verbal quotes from briefings in your press releases, brochures and advertisements.

3. **Take bad reviews of your product strategy as constructive criticism.** Analysts are paid to tell it like it is, and if they tell you to consider an exit strategy, don't be offended, you're getting free advice at this point! Think of it as a perspective you may not have even seen before.

Summary of Lessons Learned

There's been an overriding message from this book so far, and it is that honesty is the currency you trade with when it comes to working with analysts. Throughout this book you'll see how analysts also are at times not the most honest people in the world either, and they can easily get turned into big fans of specific companies only to see their shortsightedness from mistakes later. You have to however be the initiator of the level of professionalism you want to be treated with when it comes to working with analyst organizations. Consider these key points as you work with analysts and plan your strategy:

- When in doubt tell the truth always to analysts.

- Analysts realize that when everything looks too good to be true for your company and its products they typically are.

- Don't expect to have an analyst be your personal endorser as their credibility is on the line with every user of technology they recommend software, services and products to.

- Stay focused on messaging and ask for feedback often from analysts as you prepare briefing materials, presentations and concepts.

- Never rely completely on PowerPoint slides for your presentation; have the goal of mixing up the dialog and having more discussion and guidance than one-side communication. The goal is to have an interactive session not a pedantic one.

- Work to build long-term relationships by inviting analysts to participate in your closed-door strategy sessions and planning meetings.

2

Starting With The Truth

Day-In-The-Life: An Analyst Goes Overboard

Kelly Herdon's[1] career as an industry analyst had progressed from being in client service and then joining a research division of a major analyst organization known globally for its influence on IT spending in many of the world's largest corporations. He had been quick to critique the vendors in the arena he had covered even during his days in client service, which delighted the vendor and user clients he had been serving in his role over the last five years. With the greater need for coverage in databases, Kelly was given the lead analyst role for tracking database vendors. As a result, Kelly was constantly being updated on the latest product, service, and marketing directions of the world's largest and most powerful software companies. Visiting the world's most interesting cities at the request and on the tab of these software companies appealed to him as he had never left Boston before, and Kelly began to see himself as part of the market-making force for databases. His enthusiasm for each vendor's strengths in the database market was clear and when asked by companies looking for recommendations on which database to buy, Kelly had developed an informal methodology to guide clients to the best technologies.

As is sometimes the case with successful analysts, success breeds complacency. Instead of focusing on the corporations and their needs, he started really believing that he would be infallible and would always make the right technology recommendation. One corporation then another started to question his judgment as he would blindly recommend very high-end databases for tasks that a mid-tier database application could deliver. Often corporations would have pre-existing relationships with smaller vendors and Kelly would not be aware of them, endorsing the largest vendors he knew of specifically for each project. The honeymoon

---

1. The name has been changed but the situation described here happens.

8

period had gone on too long and user clients were starting to question Kelly's objectivity, especially since all the quotes he gave in the media supported the largest of vendors. One day a user client called him on his bias in the middle of a call. Kelly was at first insulted, and then the user went on saying they were using a smaller vendor's products right now and they were working out OK; which completely contradicted what Kelly had said in earlier meetings. The user client wrote a scathing note to the head of the division Kelly was a member of and the user account was eventually taken away from him.

Key take aways from this real life example:

- **Analysts go myopic from time to time.** Every analyst at one time or another has been down the road Kelly has, in varying degrees of pain from being blinded by exceptional sales and relationship skills from analyst relations professionals. When the world's most powerful business leaders and their corporations come calling on analysts it's a powerful impact.

- **It's not a question of ethics it's a question of self-awareness.** Despite what so many industry participants including vendors, press and users say that analysts are questionable when it comes to ethics the vast majority of analysts fiercely are. They would not survive for long as analysts if they were that blatantly unethical. The self-policing that is happening right now in the analyst community expunges anyone with questionable ethics.

- **Build analyst relationships like an investment, adding deposits of credibility over time.** Just as you'd build your 401K or savings account, and just as it takes time to really build anything of value, the same holds true for analyst relationships. You have to keep focusing on working with analysts as an investment as part of your global communications, analyst and public relations strategies.

Are Analysts Ethical?

Any software vendor considering spending tens of thousands to multiple hundreds of thousands of dollars with an analyst has this lingering question in the back of their minds, even if it is never said. Of course for many vendors they are hoping that the more they spend with an analyst organization the greater the:

- Payback on leads thrown their way during evaluations
- Mentions in reports and articles

- One of the founders mentions them in their writing
- Press mentions that are favorable
- Being short-listed on many different opportunities
- Being mentioned during industry events and presentations
- A practice named after the market definition you have come up for your company

These are just the start of expectations that many vendors have, and expect to get further down each of these actions and the list itself for what they pay. When analysts don't deliver on these areas and more, the worst thing to do is threaten to pull your contract or cancel the relationship. Pushing analyst firms to a pay to play mentality for higher renewal rates is just polluting the industry with lots of false expectations at best and unethical practices at worst. It's time to level the playing field of ethics in analyst relations.

Let's look at the myths that surround the ethics of analysts and clear the air.

Myth 1: The more I spend with you the more positive you will be about my products, organization, management, and execution.

This is flawed thinking on the side of vendors due to the following facts:

- **Go for a reciprocal relationship with analyst organizations no matter how small or large you are.** It's best to strike a balance between positive and negative information shared with analysts. The more you tell the truth the greater the respect.

- **Knowledge and insight are the currency that analysts trade in.** To get the most out of any analyst relations effort, get knowledge-based objectives around your strategy defined first, and consider communications objectives as part of the knowledge transfer process.

- **Analysts pride themselves on the accuracy of their recommendations to IT organization and their satisfaction figures into the size of analysts' bonuses.** If your technology is behind the market yet you spend seven figures with an analyst you won't get mentioned once for a short list. Combining innovative technology, viability in terms of financial health, and strong customer references is what really makes certain vendors stand out, regardless of their size.

Myth 2: Only the world's largest vendors get true support from analyst organizations because they write the biggest checks.

The fact is that many small vendor clients have unique technologies that align to business processes in client companies the analysts serve, and user references, innovative technology and strength of a management team mean much more than the check written to the analyst firm. Consider these points when it comes to evaluating if analysts are all simply "bought" by large vendors:

- A relatively unknown developer of routers, hubs and switches goes from relative obscurity to a household name, due to excellent marketing, strong work on distribution channels, and recommendations of analysts. Fortune Magazine covered the rise of this company during the 1990s and the integral role industry research and analysts played in the role of the company's growth. The company's name: *Cisco.*

- Apple Computer's steady rise over the last two decades is directly attributable to their analyst relations efforts of showing what's possible when a products' technological expertise meets a management team able to define quickly and clearly a vision of graphics superiority in computing. Dell Computer was always regarded as a mail order marketer and not taken seriously when it came to creating servers, storage network architectures, or workstations. In short, they were seen as a company who excelled at the essentials of what it takes to excel at mail order marketing, but clearly struggled when it came to the more advanced technology products. Since then, Dell has eclipsed competitors in each of these arenas and more, and much of their recognition of thought leadership has come from International Data Corporation (www.idc.com), Gartner (www.gartner.com) and others. Clearly the turnaround for Dell involved the analysts getting behind their vision even when the company's quarter to quarter performance showed a company in transition.

Toshiba America's Computer Systems Division growth from a $40M printer division to a $500M division selling laptop PCs, printers, servers, and PDAs was a direct result of strong marketing, excellent supply chain integration with the development facilities in Japan, and the handling of the thorny issue of one Toshiba subsidiary selling milling machine technology to the Russians. Just as Toshiba America was getting its momentum in the U.S. market, a subsidiary half a world away sold technology to the Russians that made submarines right so quiet American sonar could not detect them. Toshiba America's turnaround on this point alone is worthy of best practices in analyst and lobbyist relations. Turning what was a very destructive situation into a positive one is best practices in action when it comes to analyst relations. McKinsey & Company and the Harvard Business Review have both documented these success stories in articles published over the period of 1992 to 1999.

Myth 3: I can overcompensate for terrible service, support and products by overspending with any analyst organization.

This ranks right up there with giving a large donation to a pre-school where you want your child to go in Manhattan. Preschools are extremely competitive in Manhattan, and it's been well known that the city's elite will do whatever it takes to get their children into the best possible schools and if it means a contribution in six figures, then so be it. That's been the fodder for *The Wall Street Journal* a few years ago regarding one investment analyst that tried to assure his children a good education. While this looks entertainingly unethical, the same basic concepts apply to the way some companies think analyst relations work. Consider this worst practice in analyst relations of companies that tried and failed to make this myth a reality.

- **Selling the vision and not executing on it.** During the late 1990s and as recently as 2001 there were still small companies that had flimsy value propositions based more on the annuity models that venture capitalists liked so much during the last run-up. The fact is that many of these companies had very little if any products, light ability to execute, and a terrible sense of customer service. Many of these companies however aggressively spent on research firms to get coverage for their supposed products, and would get indignant if they did not get coverage. No analyst would touch their technologies as they were still in PowerPoint or worse yet, on whiteboards.

Myth 4: Analyst organizations need to be evaluated only on the leads they bring in.

So what's the payback of signing up with an analyst organization if they aren't going to be bringing you new business on a monthly or even a quarterly basis? Where's the ROI when analyst organizations don't bring in new business as much as your other lead management programs? Small and large vendors alike think like this, and rob themselves of so much more of the analyst relationship. Don't try to bottom-line the concept of getting great insights from analysts. Hiring one of these analysts would be a huge win for any vendor; and their advice was definitely worth at least five times the cost of an annual subscription in the cost savings their ideas generated alone.

The bottom line is that leads are an outgrowth of executing the core parts of your analyst relations strategy; they are not an end unto themselves, they are the results of working with analysts to gain their insights and get a relationship of trust created. That is a critical point. Do not ever confront an analyst about the leads they bring you or you're basically like the parents of kids in Manhattan looking to drive a pay-to-play mentality. Analysts and advisory firms lose their value when they lose their ability to influence decision makers.

Consider the following examples to see how shortsighted it is to just consider leads as the primary reason for engaging with an analyst organization. Notice that payback of these following examples show that the impact of the analyst was far over and above what any leads could deliver:

- **Research projects show lead generation without management and escalation is useless, and you can't control lead escalation inside analyst firms.** While the most of aggressive of companies will argue that they can control analysts that bring them into deals, if a user account ever even gets the hint of it, the credibility of both the analyst and the vendor is gone. How this relates to treating analysts as lead generators is that any vendor really cannot control the outcome of even being short-listed. There are too many things to control and ultimately no one controls the end user or customer.

- **Enterprise Applications Integation vendor named to shortlist for a global conglomerate.** Instead of pushing their analysts to just get them leads, a major EAI vendor took a much more patient approach and made sure the analysts they worked with had more than enough customer references to work with, the latest briefings on product updates, and also had a series of executives work with analysts to keep them informed of the latest wins and losses in the pipeline, and also provided analysts the opportunity to speak with customers at a customer advisory board. From all that work and the fact that the EAI vendor had done a tremendous job of making sure all analysts were up to date, one analyst recommended they be short-listed by a global conglomerate who was working on re-defining their entire infrastructure. Being short listed go the EAI vendor into over 22 divisions within the span of 18 months. If the approach had been just on leads the result would have been completely different.

- **You are really leasing mindshare in an analyst's mind, and once you leave another vendor steps in.** Let's face it, an analyst's brain has just so much room for tracking vendors and their many product, service, marketing and positioning strategies. Looking at an analyst organization only as the provider of leads actually hurts you, as it takes the focus away from broadening mindshare with the analyst and instead pushes the focus over to purely execution. Given a choice you want an analyst thinking more about all your strategies and how to make them work than simply creating leads.

Myth 5: A successful briefing always leads to being written about.

At the intersection of Public Relations and Analyst Relations there is the expectation that any concerted effort to members of the analyst and press community will lead to at least a press mention. This is a fallacy; realize that the analyst is in the business of providing the best guidance possible to buyers, and even if your briefing is the best one they have ever seen, without user references, without building trust with the analyst and ultimately showing your company is going to be one that survives in your chosen markets, nothing will be written much less mentioned about your company.

There is no such thing as a single briefing leading to being written about; start thinking that a briefing is just one of the many aspects of a total Analyst Relations strategy. If you come prepared to a briefing with user references that's much better, but still, the analyst needs to follow up with the references, check them out and evaluate them relative to every other company's references.

Myth 6: Analyst organizations' greatest value is in marketing tactics.

In fact the highest payback from analyst organizations is to actively contribute to your company's understanding of both tactical and strategic opportunities, including the positioning of your company for future growth.

The fact that in tough times Analyst Relations gets held to the metrics of Public Relations forces many companies to drive their analysts to be lead generators, custom quote and white paper producers, and closers on sales calls. If the analyst sees the company as capable given the buyer's requirements, lead generation and closing are a natural outgrowth.

Myth 7: Leads are the only deliverable that really matters.

Many companies drive their entire Return on Investment (ROI) for analyst relations from leads generated, often discounting the guidance given of a year or two of an engagement with the company.

It's important for companies to realize what analyst firms think when all they hear is "what leads did you get for me this year?" Sure, that is part but not all of the return generated from investing in an analyst relationship, but just centering on this shortchanges so many vendors from the other aspects of making the most of their investments in analyst organizations.

If you are in the middle of re-negotiating with an analyst firm, please don't make this the main part of your re-negotiation strategy. There are much cheaper lead generation strategies; analysts excel at guidance for both buyers and vendors, and use them that way.

Myth 8: Analysts are arrogant, difficult to approach, judging companies instead of helping them

The fear that many companies have of analysts is unfounded. There's a tendency to see any analyst organization that is not understood as arrogant, difficult to work with and approach, and too quick to judge companies.

Analysts have earned this reputation from being often highly opinionated, strongly focused on what's needed by the buyers they serve, and praised for their level of analytical insight. Some do get arrogant as a result, yet anyone running Analyst Relations and in charge of managing these relationships has got to be very clear on one point: Analysts exist to serve buyers and guide vendors. There is the issue of why any analyst firm exists, and that is to serve buyers, vendors, venture capitalists, the media and many others.

Getting to What Analysts Really Think of your Company

During hard times analyst organizations have a tendency to be more positive to vendors when they visit, hoping for renewals, higher satisfaction ratings and better overall performance measures. While you can't really blame analyst organizations for acting like this, you can find out what they really think of you by considering the following ideas and taking action on a few if not all of them. If you are getting nothing but incredibly positive feedback there is definite cause for concern as any analyst needs to report back where they see your weaknesses in addition to your strengths however.

You've got to get analysts to tell about your weaknesses as a company if you're going to improve as a company. That's what you're really paying for; the insights to what needs to change in your company.

Presented here are ideas for getting to exactly what an analyst organization thinks of you:

- **Preface every briefing by saying you will want specific, action oriented feedback.** Tell the analysts that you want their honest assessment of your content, presentation style, executives' credibility (once they are off the phone of course!) and an overall assessment of how your company stacks up to others in your industry. Ask if the briefing was useful for them, also be sure to ask if they would change anything, and if so what? You have to get the analysts to get involved with the briefing and your company to get the most out of a briefing.

- **Invite analysts to participate in the direction of your company.** This is admittedly difficult to do but very critical if you are going to get analysts to level with you. Invite them to your Advisory Board and Customer Council meetings, and also get them into your offices as much as possible to give them a chance to deliver honest feedback. You have to get analysts into situations where they can deliver honest feedback.

- **Give analysts tough problems to solve.** Giving analysts the chance to tackle tough problems and letting them know where their contributions paid off is also a great way to get honest feedback about your company. You have to find tough problems and hand them over to analysts so they have a stake in your company's success as well.

- **Invite analysts to your company's staff meetings to tell your CEO they good, bad and ugly about your company.** This also gives analysts the opportunity to get face time with your CEO and build a strong relationship. Certain analysts will be intimidated by your CEO, but its critical that the analyst sees your CEO as having skin in the game in a big way if they are going to believe in your company.

- **Use web-based questionnaires to measure how analyst organizations view you relative to your competitors.** There's just a few vendor companies doing this today, but it's very effective in getting honest, reliable and measurable feedback. One globally known company in software and services administers one of these after every product introduction. The result is that they know instantly if their positioning, differentiating messages and competitive direction are understood by the analyst community or not.

- **Ask them to write the most critical article or short commentary on your company they can think of.** As you build a relationship with an analyst it's a good idea to go and get an assessment of exactly what they think of your company's products, strategies, service record, sales record and overall growth.

Client Advisory Boards and Councils are an analyst relations' secret weapon

Treat advisory boards, councils and customer events as an opportunity to get analysts what they need most: direct conversations with your customers. Consider these key points about having analysts involved with Client Advisory Boards or Councils:

- **Validation of your overall business model by speaking about the market.** This is a powerful use of Analyst Relations; get the analysts covering your market arena to events and have them discuss the strengths, weaknesses, opportunities and threats of your company. Further, having analysts at a customer event gives them the chance to really get to know your customers, and that relationship is golden to you.

- **Make sure analysts have the chance to meet one-on-one with key customers.** One of the world's enterprise software vendors does this incredibly well. At the launch of one of their server products, they had a separate track specifically for analysts to meet with early adopters of their server applications. If you don't have an early adopter program for upcoming product introductions, consider getting one underway for your next generation of applications.

- **Ask the analyst for an assessment of the customer references at the event afterwards.** Be sure to get together with the analyst and see if the references were what they were looking for. If not, be sure to arrange more customer visits as required.

- **Send a thank you note and a small gift thanking them for their time.** This is a nice touch and shows that your company has class. Be sure to have your CEO send over a short note thanking the analyst for their time and send over something to say thank you.

Fact of Life: Analysts Have Their Favorite Vendors

Apart from all the talk of being unbiased and willing to be impartial when a company asks for advice of which technology, software application, integration technology, server, disk drive or adapter to purchase, analysts do have their favorite vendors. While many analysts and their organizations vigorously deny this is the case, there is one very important fact to remember: it is human nature to prefer one alternative over another. Do you prefer vanilla or chocolate ice cream? On a plane, window or isle? It's so fundamentally based in human nature to have preferences it is just ridiculous to say that analysts are of a higher plane of ethics that preferences do not sway them. Just accept that fact, and realize that there are analysts that have self-awareness to question their preferences. They may ask themselves "Why do I prefer larger vendors over best-of-breed?" or vice versa.

So how do you find the analysts who have the self-awareness to get to a truly ethical approach to giving guidance?

Here are a few things to look for when trying to find an honest and grounded analyst worth investing in:

- **Exceptional industry experience before being an analyst.** The best analysts have a wealth of hands-on experience, implementing software, solving problems their user clients face, and managing IT organizations. Look for a strong resume first to see the best analysts overall.

- **When they get quoted its usually controversial.** If the analysts tracking your space only say glowing things about the biggest vendors, keep looking. You want to find an analyst who has their own perspective, and the tone and independent thought in quotes will highlight that quality.

- **Seems to be selective about webinars and events**. Analysts get asked to speak on average three to five times per week, and the major analysts get asked even more than that. If you're looking for analysts who are self-aware enough to pull themselves away from being totally consumed by any vendor, watching the webinars they are and aren't in as a very good barometer.

Summary of Lessons Learned

There's the constant question of whether analysts can be bought, and if so, who owns them and for how much, and does it even make sense for smaller vendors to have an analyst relations strategy. The bottom line is that analysts do have favorite vendors and working around that takes patience. Here are some strategies to consider:

- The best two strategies in the near-term for managing analysts is to get them plenty of responsive references. So many vendors struggle with this point, but its critical to get a strong user reference program in place. It can make or break your analyst relations strategies.

- Analysts do have favorite vendors and it's your job to figure out, ethically, how to be one of them.

- Get analysts and your CEO together for honest discussions about how your company is doing in the eyes of the industry and what opportunities you may not be seeing.

- Don't treat analyst organizations as lead generation tools, as the cost per lead is huge and the opportunities for more strategy level opportunities make a single lead look miniscule.

3

Finding ROI With Analyst Organizations

Why Tough Love Matters

Never trust an analyst who doesn't give you some candid and direct feedback about your company's weaknesses, or at the very least something to work on. You are paying for constructive feedback. If for some reason you want analyst organizations to tell you everything that's *right* with your company you are wasting a ton of money. You are buying insight, not compliments.

If an analyst organization does not give you any constructive feedback and just showers you with compliments, fire them and hire a PR firm for half the money. You will get the same result.

Case studies will show you why giving and getting direct, honest and often brutally direct feedback on your company's positioning is critical. Any analyst not giving out "tough love" either has no idea of where you are strong and weak, doesn't care, or most critically, doesn't see where you can improve. This is the highest interaction with any analyst; get them to open up and critique your company for all it's weaknesses, bad decisions and lack of focus on customers, channels, new products, or when necessary, re-vamping the management team. You can find any PR firm to tell you how great your company is; the dollars you spend with an analyst organization to get highly qualified feedback on strategies and direction is what really matters.

Competent Analyst Firms: No Kumbiaya Here

Let's face it. Business is tougher than it ever has been before and the last thing you need is an analyst organization that is going to tell you that you're doing great (when back in your company's offices you wonder how to meet payroll some months worst case and if you will ever see profitability in many cases). So be cautious of the overly positive analyst who may tell you everything you want to hear in the hopes of pleasing you into renewal or into being a client. You can get people to sing your praises a lot more cheaply than just going to analyst organizations who have reputations for being highly paid yes-men and yes-women and paying them high dollar.

Any analyst organization that is not delivering tough love today needs to be looked at as an unnecessary expense and considered for trimming in the next budget cycle. Any PR organization will find you firms that will trumpet your strengths and ignore your weaknesses. Analyst organizations need to be relied on for delivering critical insights into your strategies.

Companies acquiring technology, those people you want analysts to impact, don't respect firms that are yes-men and yes-women. So be sure to take a critical eye to analyst organizations that don't deliver on the value of critical insight. Ironically this is the toughest of things to measure but the most important to track. It's clear that if the Wall Street Journal has written about research companies taking thousands of dollars to write glowing reports on technology that was not in existence or even partially done or worst of all, failed customers that purchased the applications.

The bottom line is don't have your Analyst Relations strategies end up as road kill. Use analysts for what they are really intended for: critical insights into your business and its market position, and honest feedback on how your company is doing. It's great to have strong relationships with analysts, but be sure to always end any briefing, strategy day or meeting with even more respect from analysts than when you started.

Don't go into analyst relationships and tours expecting praise and compliments; expect to hear what's wrong with your company and seek out what needs to change.

Gartner Market Scope: Worth signing up with Gartner to get in?

The Gartner Group (www.gartner.com) has re-named its Magic Quadrant the Market Scope. During the boom years of the late 1990s nearly every company that received funding or even went through an IPO had to get a Gartner subscription at a minimum, if nothing else to populate their S1s (S1 is a document you file with the Securities and Exchange Commission to register your intentions to go public) with market statistics to substantiate their market direction and position. Investors expected to at least see Gartner's figures in S1s and business plans. What this drove is many firms subscribing to Gartner and other research firms who really could not afford it but turned the Magic Quadrant into the holy grail.

Most importantly however is that information technology buyers rely on the Magic Quadrant and now the Market Scope to decide which companies are strong in the product arenas they are looking at, which are borderline and which are not worth looking at. There's the implied position of a company on the Market Scope or Quadrant that their ability to execute everything from product strategies to integration and service can be summed up in two dimensions. Many IT buyers consider the two dimensions of the Quadrant really not as useful in helping with major investments in software, services or hardware.

Don't go after Market Scope or Magic Quadrant positioning just for its own sake; get the foundation of what's necessary to be a more aggressive competitor in your markets and the requirements Gartner expects for listing on the Market Scope will fall out of those efforts.

Specifically focusing on these areas will give you competitive depth immediately and also give you market clout to go after Gartner to get listed on their graphical representation of your market space. Go after these goals and the Market Scope will follow:

- **100% or very high referencability of customers.** This is golden and can translate into sales much faster than being mentioned in a quadrant or market scope. Being listed in an analyst's report helps but analysts need referenceable customers to talk to, not knowing you are listed in another firms' graphical representation of a market.

- **Synchronizing product introductions across several geographies at the same time.** Any company capable of synchronizing the launch of their products across several countries and regions of the world at the same time clearly has the potential to be a leader in its arena. Ironically companies work for years to get onto the Magic Quadrant and now the Market Scope all the while having this capability. Ironically demonstrating this to other analyst organizations and potential clients means more to many companies than their location on a grid.

- **Alliances that are real.** Forget about the alliances that didn't earn a dime; think of the ones that really gave your company entrance into an entirely new market or opened up your existing markets more effectively than before. If you're working with a major enterprise software vendor be very specific about which area and the results you are accomplishing.

- **Strong financial performance that is verifiable even if you are private.** One of the most common questions analysts get is who is viable and who is well capitalized or not. The common techniques analysts use is to look at Dun & Bradstreet ratings, credit reports from Experian and other credit reporting agencies. Coming forward with your financial statements even under NDA is an excellent approach to prove viability of your company to analysts. It's clear that as the economy gets tougher and sales opportunities get more and more competitive to win, your best investment is in an analyst relations program that shows you as a strong and viable privately held company.

- **Strong distribution of customers by applications.** Recall that the most important attribute you can have is a trustworthy reputation with analysts and that describing which of your applications are the best selling and backing it up with numbers is critical. This not only shows that your company has a strong level of information sharing across divisions but also has a good grasp of what customers are purchasing and why. This is also one of the toughest areas companies deal with as they try to get Gartner to include them on Market Scopes or its predecessor the Magic Quadrant.

Why Analyst Relations Is an Investment Not an Expense

The approach your company takes to building an Analyst Relations strategy needs to be completely different than a Public Relations or marketing strategy. For many companies, you may find that Analyst Relations is part of product marketing, product management, or even included in Public Relations.

For many vendors, working with analyst relations expert firms including Lighthouse Analyst Relations (www.lighthousear.com), Knowledge Capital Group (www.knowledgecap.com), and Tekrati (www.tekrati.com) has given companies the ability to accomplish an even higher ROI given the fact these firms have expertise gained from years of experience in this field. Tekrati is a great website to track the analyst industry as well; it is full of valuable information and is a must-visit site at least once a week if you are in Analyst Relations or Public Relations. I've had great experiences working with Lighthouse Analyst Relations; very responsive and a great depth of expertise in the area of high tech analyst relations. Duncan Chapple, Managing Principal—Europe, Middle East, and Africa at Lighthouse Analyst Relations does an excellent job of managing global analyst relations strategies from Europe. Overall, these firms excel at the project management aspects of analyst relations and are definitely worth considering if you choose to outsource, or look for insights and guidance in analyst relations.

Analyst Relations Is The Equity Of Your Company

Any Public Relations, Marketing, Product Marketing vice president or even Chief Marketing Officers reading this will argue that Analyst Relations needs to be interlocked with and coordinated to the broader plans of a Public Relations, product development, and product marketing effort. That's certainly true, yet Analyst Relations needs to have its own key performance indicators (KPIs) or metrics of performance. The following is a comparison of the measures of performance AR functions gets measured on relative to PR functions and the focus of AR versus PR in many companies.

Table 3-1:
Comparing Analyst and Public Relations Functions

Comparing strategy dimensions	Analyst Relations	Public Relations
Time focus of projects	Strategic and long-term	Tactical and focused on 90–120 day time horizons
Lead count expectations	Very few compared to other lead generation strategies	Thousands. Problem is qualifying and following up on them.
Number of leads delivered per year	20–30*	10,000 to 1,000,000
Cost per lead	Very high	Lower the better
Number of press mentions	25–250	1,000 to 10,000; this is one of the many metrics that PR gets measured on.
Strategy sessions with senior management	8 per year is recommended where analysts are brought in	3–4 mostly on PR strategy

Table 3-1:
Comparing Analyst and Public Relations Functions (Continued)

Comparing strategy dimensions	Analyst Relations	Public Relations
Brown Bag Universities for product management	1 per month with different analysts brought in to give senior and product management insights into the direction of the industry	1 every six months on the direction of PR
Competitive positioning feedback	Continuously	Based on reviews from journalists; relies on AR for competitive updates
Exit Strategies	Specializes on assisting companies with their exit strategies from consolidating markets; shrinking product areas.	Not covered in detail; more on execution of an exit strategy once it's decided

*   This is typical for an information technologies vendor with between 65–120 customers already and a stable product strategy with distribution of customers throughout all products. The difference is that many of these leads from analyst organizations are highly qualified in the buying cycle.

Clearly each of these functions in a company has the potential to make major contributions. Table 3-1 shows how Analyst Relations gets measured relative to Public Relations. Both have critical roles in a company yet Analyst Relations needs to have the freedom to invest in long-term relationships to get the results they need. It's all about building equity in relationships with analysts; that is the critical take-away. There are the issues of leads, press mentions and number of times mentioned in print including reports, but that's clearly only the by-product of a strong relationships with analysts already.

Measuring the ROI of Analyst Organizations

Any ROI analysis starts with the costs of the investment versus the benefits obtained. For purposes of this example the following assumptions are made:

Investment per year:

- Average cost per analyst firm subscription (2 firms): $70,000
- Manager of Analyst Relations (burdened cost) $95,000
- Travel and Entertainment for year of AR functions $15,000
- Strategy Sessions with several firms $10,000
  Total Budget for Analyst Relations: **$190,000**

Returns from analyst organizations:

- Merger and acqusition guidance for senior executives[1] $10,000
- Cost savings from feedback on existing consolidating markets[2] $50,000
- Short-listed in ten opportunities[3] $90,000
- Five shorted listed buyers purchase from vendor[4] $600,000
- Proactive data on new market developments[5] $75,000
  Total Benefits from an Analyst Relations Strategy: **$775,000**

Return on Investment: $775,000/$190,000 = 245%

Assumptions:

1. The going rate for a full day strategy session with a senior director of research. This includes guidance on companies targeted for acquisition.

2. Recommendation to discontinue products that are in consolidating marketplaces. Savings based on the costs of a saved product introduction.

3. Fully burdened cost of a sales representative to work ten accounts and get short-listed over 12 months.

4. Analysts' recommendations get your company into five deals your company wins. This assumes the average deal size is $150,000 for a mid-sized enterprise hardware or software vendor.

5. The cost of replacing an analyst service with one additional headcount to track your industry sector full-time for one year. This is a fully burdened cost for another headcount in your company for example.

Summary of Lessons Learned

When companies think about the ROI of their analyst relations efforts they inevitably only think of their expenses and not the benefits. But in re-evaluating analyst investments its critical to look at the long-term implications of having analysts know your C-level executives well; it's more about building up equity with analyst organizations. There's more to having and on-again off-again relationship with an analyst organization, and if your company is going to get the benefits of having analysts tracking your company you need to be consistent.

Additional take-aways from this chapter include:

- Every dollar you invest in analyst relations has a direct impact on the insights your company gets into the direction of the markets you compete in. The alternative to having an analyst relations program with outside firms is to build the processes inside your company. With headcount being at a premium many companies are finding this tough to do.

- Get past ROI as just being lead generation and get analysts and your CEO together for strategy sessions.

- Getting short-listed by an analyst has everything to do with proving your company can execute. This translates into getting analysts customer references early and often.

- If any analyst firm you are contracted with does not give you direct feedback consider dropping them for the ones that give you more honesty on your company and how it is perceived.

- If your company is going through headcount reductions, consider outsourcing analyst relations to one of the following firms. Knowledge Capital Group, Lighthouse Analyst Relations or Tekrati are all excellent, and of these three, Lighthouse Analyst Relations has proven its responsiveness in interactions with vendors I've worked with.

4

Best and Worst Practices of Analyst Tours and Visits

Case Study: Aggressive Listening Pays Off

When one of the leading enterprise software vendors rolls into Boston, analyst expect lots of meetings, even more PowerPoint, and dinner meetings that are full of what's going on in the core areas of their businesses. But one software vendor has transcended the grind of analyst tours by being able to deliver quickly what's needed most by analysts: customer references and verifiable business results delivered using their software. There are PowerPoint slides decks, yet only the first ten slides are on product vision, features and benefits and the remainder is all about customer success stories and the hard numbers of results they are delivering. This is the most powerful of all and really what analysts in every firm needed; validation and customers willing to talk about those successes. Armed with such strong presentations materials, the analyst team hit the road.

With such great briefing materials any member of the executive or Analyst Relations team could easily have gone into lecturing analysts, one by one, as they made the rounds of the various firms. But something else happened. The slides rarely were shown and when they were it was about a specific customers—and fast forwarding three months, specific reports relevant to the customers had them and the enterprise vendor listed.

Let's look at how this enterprise vendor was able to get to this level of performance with analyst firms:

1. **It took over two years of listening to what analysts needed and delivering**. There was over two years since the first series of meetings with this specific set of analyst relations people on the enterprise vendors' side and the analysts who tracked them. Analysts had routinely

questioned the vendors' ability to deliver in areas other than their core business, like CRM for example, and while this made life for the analyst relations people pretty tough internally, they stuck with a strategy of delivering references and keeping the propaganda to a minimum.

2. **Becoming a relevant vendor takes time.** You can't slam through pages and pages of PowerPoint and hope to convince analysts by sheer volume of materials you are a vendor to write about. Instead what you don't say—about how wonderful you and your company are, about how no customers are unhappy—or other stretches of the truth—will get you there. Being relevant to an analyst firm is not like getting accepted into some exclusive country club, it's about earning your way through pure performance onto a starting line-up for a debate or athletic team.

3. **CEO to Senior Analyst, VPs and CEO summits regularly happened.** This is where aggressive listening really took hold. The CEO of this enterprise vendor actually listened to the analysts, senior analysts, even the CEOs of the analyst firms. Not so much just to appease them but to sincerely explain strategies and seek guidance. Alliances were born at an interpersonal level and strong relationships resulted. Relevance happened over time because the relationships grew stronger and more and more information was shared.

4. **Analysts did not revert to pay-for-play.** On the surface it's easy to make a snap judgment that the analyst firms sold out to the enterprise vendor and nothing but positive press happened in quotes, articles, and reports. Nothing could be further from the truth; in fact there have been times in this specific relationship where the more outspoken analysts have continued to slam this vendor's product architecture prompting a call from one CEO to another that has turned heated at times. All this is critical for the analyst firm to retain its most prized asset—it's credibility—and the vendor gets honesty and not just parroted-back responses they could pay anyone to produce.

5. **The milestones in the relationship are all about listening and responding to each other.** It has nothing to do with the size of the subscription of this vendor with the analyst firm and everything to do with how relevant they are to the users of technology the analyst firms serve. The enterprise vendor didn't buy their way into good graces with the company; they showed over time that they took the advice of the analyst

firm both in small decisions, and when they trusted the analyst firm, in larger and larger decisions. The reciprocal relationship of the two companies has grown over the year. The bottom line is that the milestones that mark the relationship are defined by reciprocal actions on both sides.

Bottom line: It makes no difference how large or small your company is, but how hard you work to stay relevant to your customers. The analysts have to follow what's successful, and if you become even more successful with your strategies based on analyst's guidance, then you're in a position to build a strong, reciprocal relationship with analysts. Earn analysts' respect, don't try to buy it. And that's at the heart of what happened with the enterprise vendor and aggressive listening: they earned respect by not trying to buy their way out of trouble but by earning respect by listening to what analysts had to say, taking what was valuable for their application areas, and moving forward.

What Best Practices in Analyst Tours Looks Like

Companies that excel at analyst tours execute strongly on the following tasks, dimensions and goals. Notice that there are measures of performance or Key Performance Indicators (KPIs) as well, and the best companies do much more rigorous work on their Analyst Relations strategies internally to make sure there is a common frame of reference given to each and every analyst firm. Companies accomplishing best practices do the following:

- **Make the CEO accessible, accountable, and actively involved in every tour.** With how many companies analysts track and the very few vendors that get their CEOs out on the road for these tours, it's a rare treat to get a chance to discuss a company with the person responsible for all of it. In these difficult economic times there are so many companies trying to go in several directions at once, and often analysts want to know what's the top priority, what's secondary and what's working or not. Most importantly when it comes for an analyst recommending your company to a buyer, it helps to have assurance directly from the CEO that your product strategies are going to be constant. It is by far the most competitively advantageous action to take with analysts: get the CEO out early and often and get relationships going. Ultimately the analysts will trust product direction and recommend the company if the CEO is willing to stake their credibility on it.

- **Send customer references before all briefings and visits.** Customer references are the currency you trade with analyst firms with. With strong references and the ability to deliver contact information quickly, analysts will have the opportunity to speak with your references before the meetings with you and your team.

- **Deliver a thought-provoking agenda over pounds of PowerPoint.** Challenge the analysts with a well thought out agenda that asks for guidance on new product initiatives, positioning of your company and its products relative to competition, in-detail discussions of what buyers are saying about the market arena they are in and specifically if there is any feedback from references or your other clients that the analysts may have spoken to, and what's the direction for consolidation in your segments.

- **If you use PowerPoint as a placeholder for discussions, less is more.** Companies that deliver best practices in AR take the number of slides they are going to send to analysts and cut them in half, relying on insightful yet analytical slides and key discussion points on slides themselves. Be focused on starting a discussion not dominating it. One in ten companies has gotten to the point of sending only fifteen slides or less yet can keep a discussion going for ninety minutes or more.

- **Turning dinners with analysts into a secret weapon.** This is a delicate area that many analysts and companies struggle with yet done well, this can turn into a great weapon for getting mindshare with targeted analysts in the most competitive of industries. Analysts are not obligated to attend dinners, but for companies that have people who are enjoyable to be with, vendors with interesting technology, and vendors analysts want to know more about. Keep these key points in mind if you invite an analyst to dinner and they accept:

  - **Set the goal of getting to know the analysts as people.**

  - **The following are prohibited from analyst dinners: printed presentations, laptops, press releases and reports edited to your company's advantage.**

Worst Practices in Analyst Tours: How To Avoid Being The Vendor From Hell

Consider these to be the actions that can cause an analyst to ignore or worse yet, discount your capabilities to buyers who are looking for applications, products or services in your market arena.

- **Kill Your Acronyms.** These three and four letter jumbles of letters are the shorthand of how you run your business, but they are meaningless and confusing for anyone else. For analysts that know your company well you can use them sparingly, but don't ever use acronyms when someone who doesn't know your company very well is present. It completely leaves any analyst not familiar with your firm in the dark. In general the more acronyms you can kill in your vocabulary and especially in your presentations the better.

- **Too little time allocated to each visit.** Go after the quality of the briefing you're doing, especially if it is in person. At a minimum ask for 45 minutes to 1 hour with an analyst when you visit on a tour. Trying to squeeze in too many visits in to any given day of a tour makes each briefing rushed and often gets key points left out of the conversation.

- **No executives in your company behind the products or initiatives you're briefing on.** While you and your PR team may know it, over time the analysts will know it as well. While there is pressure in a company to get the word out on any new product introduction, it's best to only invest in analyst briefings if your company is completely behind a product. Anything less is a waste of yours and the analyst's time.

- **Dial-in and Webex not defined for anyone dialing in.** Take a few minutes and get a dial-in and Webex created for any visit where you're going to have to brief analysts who are in other locations besides corporate headquarters.

Are You Delivering Best or Worst Practices?

There's no universal definition of best or worst practices, each is a matter of degrees for each company. The degrees of performance towards best practices for companies doing analyst tours and visits include the following questions. Go through the list of questions below and be honest about the reaction of analysts to your company. Worst practices is clearly answering "no" to the majority of questions below.

1. **Analysts write and ask for your white papers, customer references and technical papers and your company follows up in 48 hours.**

   Yes   No

2. **Presentations for the briefings sent a week or more ahead of time?**

   Yes   No

3. **Presented only research results from the research company you visited?**

   Yes   No

4. **Brought along C-level executives or founders?**

   Yes   No

5. **Created agendas specific to each analyst firm you visited?**

   Yes   No

6. **Killed all acronyms in your presentations?**

   Yes   No

7. **Arrived on time or early for each analyst visit?**

   Yes   No

8. **Delivered customer references before the briefings and visits.**

   Yes   No

9. **Webex and dial-ins set up a week before each briefing for remote sites.**

   Yes   No

10. **Briefing book for all executives on the tour have biographies and recent writing from the analysts being visited.**

    Yes   No

11. **Prep meetings with executives prior to tours and visits on product and company messages.**

Yes   No

Lessons Learned

The most important fact to remember when your company goes out for an analyst tour is that every day analysts gets blasted information at them and the only path to differentiation is to build reciprocal relationships where you work with them. Here are additional lessons learned from analyst tours and visits:

- Don't do an analyst tour without having a senior executive along (the more senior the better) to show that your company takes these tours and appointments seriously.

- Erase acronyms from your slides before your briefings. If no one knows what they mean outside your company you'll get the reputation of being inward centered and not focused on the outside markets.

- Define goals for each analyst visit depending on the strengths of the specific analyst firm you are going after.

- Be considerate about the analyst's time and arrive early, prepared, with the Webex and login information distributed before you arrive.

- Be very prompt on follow-up as the majority of companies either don't follow up or take weeks to get back to analysts. It's best to over-achieve on responsiveness.

5

Every Analyst Loves a CEO Who Has Passion

Day-in-the-Life: A CEO Makes an Impact in Boston

Software company CEOs run the gamut of pure technologists to pure salesmen, with every variation in marketing, sales, development or service strengths in between. What then sets a CEO's or a C-level executives' performance apart from others when they visit analysts? Here's a case in point of one that has made a big impact on the industry and financial analyst community.

Greg Michelson[1] was one of the founders of one of the fastest growing software companies in the analytics marketplace, and was constantly on the road, visiting both clients and prospects, supporting the sales force in key deals and very visible in the industry press. In short. Mr. Michelson had found his niche, and his passion was his company. He averaged 50% of every month on the road and was a fixture at conferences, often doing keynotes and also panels. What really set him apart was the candor and truth he spoke with, and when he had to spin a story for his company, did it with honesty and directness.

What really set him apart however was the ability to be brutally honest with analysts, telling them the strengths, weaknesses, future plans, concerns and questions for the future. In short, he really was after respect from analysts, and instead of lying to them, trying to deceive them or even ingratiate himself to them with promises of exclusive trips to user events, Michelson had tremendous memory where he could discuss by customer the payback each had received with his company's products. He could talk in detail where global outsourcing worked well, where it didn't, and why. Further, the rage over mergers and acquisitions was

---

1.   This is an actual example with a fictitious name inserted.

always the favorite subject of analysts, and while Michelson's company had been both the target of and had done over a dozen acquisitions in the last five years he rarely spoke in detail of this area. Instead he had more of a focus on the customer base, its changing requirements and the fact that he would have to make sure technology stayed current.

Before you dismiss this example as the dream of an analyst who needs all this data and more to serve user accounts, consider the fact that CEOs really do exist with these properties and more. If you're about to have your CEO go out on an analyst tour, consider these points, and if you can't really say "yes" to the majority of them, consider sending over another C-level executive or VP instead:

- **Has a passion for delivering results and ROI to customers.** This is something no one can fake; it is really so critical to the credibility of your CEO internally and externally that if your CEO has it, great, you will at least have the attention of both industry and financial analysts on tours. If your CEO can't really discuss in detail the ROI and results that customers are receiving, bring someone on analyst tours that can.

- **Less on whom you know and more on what you know.** Nobody likes an arrogant CEO that comes in to a briefing and starts name dropping, because this has the exact opposite effect on analysts. Worst of all never drop the name of the CEO, C-level, or VP-level members of the analyst organization and imply that since you know them you deserve special treatment.

- **In-depth knowledge of the sales pipeline.** It's surprising how many CEOs have no idea what the pipelines of their companies are, and worse, who in the pipeline is a repeat customer or not. Yet this level of detail is critical for not only managing industry and financial analysts, but in handling complex sales cycles and keeping the sales force focused. It is amazing when you find a CEO these days not familiar with what is in their company's pipelines.

- **Explains the product strategy clearly and from the customers' standpoint.** It's clear that the best CEOs at analyst relations have a firm grounding in the product vision of their companies, even if they are not the founders of the company. This kind of a CEO understands, nearly to the point of it appearing intuitive, what his company's customers think of the substitute solutions, and what the company he works for has to provide in the way of additional services, features, post-sales support, and on occasion, pricing, to make a difference in the minds of these prospects and generate sales. If this makes a CEO sound more like sales manager, they are—in fact the best ones mix leadership in management and in sales at the same time.

- **Can define the global outsourcing strategy of your company.** Nearly every company today has a global outsourcing strategy for either the development of their applications, production of their products, or the outsourcing of their call centers. A CEO needs to know about the specific projects underway and if they are successful, why. For many CEOs the unsuccessful outsourcing attempts are considered an embarrassment and something to be hidden. Outsourcing costs companies millions of dollars to pursue and in an age of total accountability there is no doubt there is either such a resounding pain in the company that needs to be resolved, or an intricate ROI analysis completed. In some companies, both are done. So when a CEO makes the annual or semi-annual trip to see the analysts, that type of analysis and insight into why the company outsourced what they did is at the top of mind for many analysts. Come prepared to talk about not only you successes but your failures as well. Nothing is more aggravating than catching a CEO in a lie about their outsourcing wins or losses, especially when what they say contradicts what is said in 10Qs filed with the S.E.C. So be honest even if you have to admit a million dollar mistake.

- **Doesn't have a cult-like approach to relating with analysts.** There are those CEOs that really have a hard time with the value proposition of an analyst firm. The thought process starts with "we are paying them, we are a customers, therefore all negative things about us—even indictments and audits by the government—should stay private and not be written about, and only our strengths should be broadcasted." That's a fallacy and a sure sign any CEO enforcing these thoughts in their analyst relations team wants a cult and not a company. It's the job of analysts to guide the acquirers of technology to the best match, and that holds true regardless of the business model of the analyst or advisory firm. So demanding that questionable business practices and run-ins with the S.E.C. or their own auditors not be written about is a disservice to everyone. What amazed me was how much CEOs and their staffs tried to cover up publicly-available information on the bad situations companies had gone through. Before every major briefing with a CEO of a publicly-held company I would read their last three 10Qs and the latest 10K on file with the S.E.C. and that pretty much laid out all the financial, legal, outsourcing, sales, marketing, production and operations challenges the companies had faced.

Why Passion in a CEO is Critical

The CEO's profile that starts out this chapter shows what happens when a CEO is a passionate leader of the company he or she is responsible for and is willing to do whatever it takes to back it up. If it means flying all night to be at client sites and then another night of flying to be at a conference, that's what they do. They are tireless in their pursuit of the passion of serving customers. Analysts love CEOs like this because their passion is all consuming and their work ethic is so commendable. They are not about the title, they are about being so ingrained in accomplishing things their efforts blend with the company. It's as if these leaders are just consumed with a vision of what they are trying to turn their companies into.

That passion is what will make or break any analyst relationship in the long-term. If you are looking to make a deposit in the equity of your analyst relationships, then getting a CEO with this level of intensity in front of analysts is critical.

On the other hand if your CEO is more of a deal-maker and sits in their cubicle or office just trying to do deals all day and hasn't been to see any of your customers in over six months, leave them home for the analyst tours. Why? Because they will have nothing that interesting to say about customers. If all you want is an M & A discussion with an analyst firm do that over the phone. Get to the heart of why you have an analyst firm on subscription in the first place: to get new ideas and insights into how to attack markets you may not heard of before, and also to create entirely new markets that your company has the potential to capture. Just spouting off about their own accomplishments and treating the analyst as if they are a captive audience is just a horrible waste of time for your CEO and the analyst. No passion in your CEO for customers and the business = no analyst tours. Send out the VP who has the best presentation skills and depth of product knowledge because that person will at least have a heartbeat of passion for the company and their work within it.

Does your CEO have passion?

If there is one burning question on every employee's mind during these tough economic times is "Does my CEO care as much about this company and my job as I do?" While the CEO may have invested themselves publically in the company, every employee, especially product managers, sales directors and VPs and most of all, analyst and financial investor relations people toss and turn at night grappling with that question. Out of the abundance of the heart, the mouth speaks. So what's coming out of your CEO's mouth? In front of industry and financial analysts? In front of customers? What's real and what isn't, and underscoring it all, where's the passion, the burning vision of serving customers with ruthless execution and strong commitment to customers and profitability or is your CEO a deal maker? So many questions and so little time but such a critical link in the chain of value you deliver to analysts, you need to manage your CEO like a valuable resource. Think laser-precision surgery, not shotgun pellets of information to see what sticks. If you trot the CEO out for the financial and industry analysts, everything had better stick.

Here are the characteristics of CEOs that have skin in the game and the credibility to go with it. Be sure your CEO has these qualities and more, and they will be a hit on analyst tours.

- **Your CEO has visited over ten clients in the last three months.** Always remember that the customer references you have is the currency you trade with to gain credibility with analysts. If your CEO has a passion for really understanding clients, then bring them along; they will be useful with analysts who want to drill into the specifics of how your products and services are being used by clients.

- **Your CEO has a genuine passion for the company's products and services.** This is impossible to fake and is so powerful for any analyst visit. If your CEO has this quality get them on the analyst tours as much as you can. If your CEO is somewhat introverted and not prone to show enthusiasm or emotion, find someone in the company that is.

- **Is honest with analysts.** This sounds so simple but it is just so lacking, the disarming honesty of a CEO to really just lay out the truth and tell it like it is. For some reason CEOs feel they are not being "CEO enough" unless they appear stilted, scripted, and totally in control—all the things are just flow from confidence and really knowing what you're talking about.

- **Has an M & A strategy that makes sense.** It's surprising how many CEOs have this grand vision of being $1B in revenue through a combination of mergers, acquisitions, and deals. This is a great jump-off point for analysts to give their feedback on M & A strategies in your company. If you have an NDA in place with the analyst firms you're visiting, be sure to get your M & A strategy documents to the analysts you're visiting before visiting them.

- **Actually reads the analysts' work you are visiting and cites their work in presentations.** Instead of seeing this as ego-stroking analysts, think of it as making an investment in a relationship with the analyst. There is a difference. By having your CEO schooled on each of the analysts' current research, insights can be more quickly gained and best of all, the analyst sees your company as receptive to their research. Getting analysts to have skin in the game when it comes to your strategies, messaging, and competitive intelligence is critical.

- **When your CEO is involved think "ROI of Analysts" constantly.** The reason for this is that next year or the following one your CEO will ask you, when you show up with an invoice from any analyst firm, what your company generated in terms of revenue, greater market or business development, or greater competitive advantage as a result. Chapter 6, Managing Analyst Relations to a Scorecard, explains how to track the contributions and performance of analyst firms. Keep in mind this isn't like hiring a lead generation firm, it's more about investing in a long-term relationship. The managing of equity in analyst relationships is critical if they are going to work—and that takes years of building. Chapter 6 describes both short-term and long-term wins.

Lessons Learned

If you run Analyst Relations or Public Relations, start thinking about your executive team as a manager of a sports team thinks about his players. Who's the best performer on the executive team? Who connects often with analysts and just nails briefings with sincerity and passion? If you are lucky it's the CEO. Think of the starters on your executive team and who you will send into which situation. The allegory of choosing where to put your best talent is equally true when it comes to dealing with the loaded questions and tough sessions analysts can dish out just as much as facing opponents during a game or match. You need executives that can face that pressure and perform for the company.

At the center of this chapter is whether your CEO has passion for their job or not—does he or she really care about the company, its customers, and its opportunities—or is this just a career layover until a better position comes along? Here are some thoughts to keep in mind when getting your CEO off the bench and into the game of working with both financial and industry analysts:

- **CEOs, in general, wonder why analyst firms are worth it.** The fact that CEOs want to see what revenue dollars that get generated from public relations and analyst relations budgets stretches the level of what CEOs are typically willing to pay for anyway, but in an era of where there is lots of demand for clear accountability even for pipeline-enabling functions like public relations just makes the job of getting yearly subscriptions approved that much more difficult.

- **Does your CEO know passion or have no more passion?** This is critical as there isn't much room left for vacillating back and forth on getting work done, results delivered and in short injecting life into a company. Either the CEO has a passion for the company or its direction or they don't. And this is unmistakable if it is there and just as noticeable if it is not. Don't ever bring a CEO on an analyst tour who doesn't have any passion for what they do. Sure, they may be great at the fine-tuning of your company but without passion for what they are doing they will not convince anyone else to really care.

- **Make sure to summarize the key results from analysts and periodically pass them by your CEO.** The next chapter is dedicated to the concept of tracking performance of analyst firms with scorecards. Think of how you present analyst results and work to your CEO as all part of setting the stage for a renewal. Because even if your CEO has not been explicit about the ROI from analysts, rest assured that conversation is coming.

- **Decide right now if your CEO is an asset or liability when it comes to working with analysts.** You know this intuitively right now if you are in Analyst or Public Relations—if you're in Investor Relations in a publicly-held company you definitely know this from quarterly conference calls. If you decide the CEO isn't a good fit then get another C-level executive or a VP designated as the analyst go-to person.

6

Managing Analysts Relations to a Score Card

Too often companies are not prepared when renewal cycles come along with the research organizations they have subscriptions with to negotiate to their best advantage. Rarely does a company take the time to actually create a scorecard, populate it with both 360-degree feedback of how the research firms have performed for the marketing, product management, public relations, investor relations, engineering and even sales forces via webinars and in-person speaking arrangements.

You have to get in the mindset that at every subscription renewal time it's time to deliver a performance review to your analyst organizations. It's time to deal out some tough love about what has gone well and what's been a disappointment. Before you start saying that you just have to have a given firm, think again. Every analyst firm is now under a microscope for ethics due to a few of the world's best-known analyst organizations being caught red-handed writing recommendations that favor the world's largest corporations. Instead of being ethical and taking a far less profitable yet infinitely more valuable road for their clients, well-known and often-quoted firms are feeling the heat for writing glowing reviews of software, hardware or services that really doesn't deliver the total cost of ownership, costs savings, or performance as portrayed. This is the new reality for analyst organizations—this critical focus is their new mode of operation. Now throw in the economics of getting CIOs and IT Departments to renew, the user accounts as they are called, whose budgets have been pinched and trimmed to lower levels than ever before. What this all adds up to is an environment where research firms must prove their value in every interaction, every briefing, every document delivered, to survive. This intensity is the only path to survival for any research firm.

Vendors re-negotiating with an analyst firm keep in mind the conditions just mentioned are the new reality for the firms you're dealing with. Chances are there have already been layoffs in parts of their organization, definitely attrition in the analyst ranks, and at the very least, challenges to growing the business as had been possible in the past.

All these dynamics create an entirely new climate when it comes to managing the relationships with analyst firms and the results you get from them. Accountability of results is now everything, and to get any kind of traction with your internal efforts to keep analyst relations humming along you need to manage analysts to goals and objectives. Now some may balk at this concept but there are several areas of analyst relationships you may not have even explored before which are quantifiable, and could contribute to the overall ROI of the relationship.

Scoring Analysts On Performance

Making investments in analysts pay off requires measuring the value—and while many analyst firms would actively and vigorously debate this it's the truth. Analysts do deliver value, and it's your job if you manage relationships to get to common ground as quickly as you can with regard to what you will be measuring them on. Figure 6-1 shows an example of an analyst scorecard.

Figure 6-1: Example of an Analyst's Scorecard

Goals and Objectives	Your Company's Response	Research firm's response	Comments	Date Due
Analyst Day at HQ	Planning a user summit to align with analyst day to make it worthwhile for research firms	Four of the six analyst firms have agreed to attend as of 9/15.	Goal is to provide users for analyst's questions and research efforts.	10/15 event day

Figure 6-1: Example of an Analyst's Scorecard (Continued)

Goals and Objectives	Your Company's Response	Research firm's response	Comments	Date Due
Mention in news flashes and reports	Research firm has been given 10 references in the last eight months; all have been followed up on	Report mentions: three customers mentioned and we're mentioned once; short articles: one mention	Conversion of customer references to mentions is 40%.	Hoping for two mentions in 12/15 report to get conversion rate to 60%
Short-listed and long-listed into opportunities	GSA and APAC Inc; referred by analysts	Cannot provide this information; have long-listed us in several opportunities but cannot tell which accounts	Against the policy of analyst firms to deliver this info; hearing from prospects themselves.	Ongoing
Prospects asking for 3rd party validation	Scheduled with sales managers	Analysts are adamant they will give best response for the user account.	Risk of sales cycles going to competitors; but analysts can validate direction	By 9/30 and fiscal close of the year
Quoted by analysts in industry magazines	26 times in the last 18 months	Push on user references is starting to pay off	Industry round-ups starting to mention us; including analyst quotes.	Ongoing work in conjunction with PR Teams
User references for upcoming report on SOX Compliance	Provided five different customers who have completed installs.	Three of the five references have been followed up on	Feedback from the customers contacted is that interviews were balanced and fair.	12/15 report due date: December is publication date for report; hoping for two user mentions.

Figure 6-1: Example of an Analyst's Scorecard (Continued)

Goals and Objectives	Your Company's Response	Research firm's response	Comments	Date Due
Vertical Market Strategy Session	Scheduled the first week of September	Providing analyst for the day of September 14th	Agenda and SWOT Analysis definition	9/23
SOX Webinar	Scheduled for Oct	Prepping content and have banner	Signed up lead analyst on SOX	Scheduled for 10/15
White Paper Series on vertical market wins.	Scheduled for production in Calendar Q4.	Analyst firms agreed to review but not write.	Need clarification on SOX market.	12/31—all three white papers delivered.

Choosing Strategies That Are Measurable

The mistake many vendor companies make when they sign up with an analyst firm is not thinking about measuring the value of the relationship over time. What's important is to select plans and strategies that really lend themselves to measurement. The following are a series of strategies that vendors use to get support for analyst firms while at the same time measuring their impact:

- **Strong customer reference programs always deliver ROI.** If there is nothing else you work on with analyst firms, this needs to be your top priority. Regardless of the approach of each analyst firm when it comes to generating revenue, the importance of user's insights and their use of key applications, technologies and services will be the most important factor for the foreseeable future. That's the core of any strong research effort—what's going on with users of technology.

  - **Build an incentive program for your sales and support team that quantifies customer performance.** Incent customers by offering to benchmark your performance relative to their goals, and in the process you can generate exactly the measures of performance you need to provide to analysts. This works very well for the companies serving customers who don't have highly confidential customer deployments.

  - **Deliver an index of performance and back it up with individual company performance.** Think about creating an index of performance for each of the application suites you sell, and develop a time series index that shows over time how you have done as a vendor in delivering value.

- **Strive for 100% customer referencability.** Even if you get to 50% that's better than many vendors and their ability to get analysts connected with customers. This is truly the currency you trade with when it comes to working with analysts, so the higher this figure the better.

- **Analyst days where your customers and analysts are invited to a summit or major event.** Many vendors are finding that these analyst days serve an incredibly useful purpose, and that is getting analysts connected with customers on a first-name basis. While I've been to many of these, the best are ones where the customers present how the company's applications, products, or services significantly contributed to a company's business goals. The ability of a vendor to routinely and significantly impact the business processes of another company is what analysts are looking for. Where the solid returns of this activity come into existence when the users were one-on-one with the analysts and told the good and bad. That was invaluable.

- **Editing, not writing, white papers is high ROI activity.** There are plenty of analyst firms out there that will write a complete white paper for you. Why then do this internally? Because you want to generate and retain the knowledge internally. Sure, you can pay any analyst firm who does this $5,000 on average, but why not just do this yourself and have the analysts proof it? That makes much more sense you save the costs of the white paper but also gets the critical knowledge included in the company. Consider this alternative, because you can have many more white papers produced using this approach versus paying for each one. And the true bottom line of this: if you pay to have the white paper written instead of writing it yourself only a handful of people in your company will understand it.

- **Webinars for lead generation that combine analysts and customers**. For most software companies the sign-ups range from just over 50 to as many as 500 depending on the topic, how pervasively promoted the webinar is, and who the speaker is. It's one of the best lead generation strategies you can use, and is by nature quantifiable. It's gratifying as well from an analyst standpoint to hear that your work has resulted in a client winning a new client, initially interested in their solution from a webinar. The focus needs to be on the business processes streamlined with the application, and while the analyst can speak to the general market direction and dynamics, leave it to the customers you have presenting on the call to trumpet your benefits. That just means a lot more than having an analyst, who may or may not have ever been in a user capacity; speak to the strengths of your application.

- **Long-listed in specific opportunities.** For many C-level executives this is the real reason they sign up with an analyst firm, and the ability of different analyst firms varies in their ability to report back results, yet you should ask at least how many times you've been long-listed in the last year. No analyst firm however will report who you were long-listed to however.

To understand the impact of analysts on your sales cycles, performing your own win/loss analysis is critical. Instead of trying to pry out the names of the research firm's clients where you have been long-listed or even short-listed, perform your own win/loss analysis. This kind of work with clients you lost will bring up competitive strengths and with enough work you could very well find out that a series of industry analysts your prospects rely on see your applications as better suited for another need. Alternatively you may be winning business and not even know it as a result of analyst relations—and that level of ROI can guarantee spending for the next year on analyst subscriptions!

Analysts Who Know Users Deliver ROI

Each analyst firm has a slightly different business model, but in general the analyst firms that have a significant percentage of their revenue from user accounts are more involved with the selection of new applications, technologies, and services. And while there are thousands of industry analysts who are heads-down on market forecasts and doing quantitative analysis of markets, there are a set of analysts who spend over 50% of their time talking with users about their needs. This is the analyst group you need to target to get any lasting ROI out of your investments in analyst firms. These are the analysts who control what gets bought, why, by who, and what you need to do as a company to make your strategies align with those needs. For technology users, these user-centered analysts are the ones that are the sounding boards on technology you need.

Not to take anything away from the thousands of analysts who crunch numbers and do forecasts—and cover vendors and entire market areas in great depth—but users are where the action is when it comes to truly outstanding research data. Finding these analysts who are serving users takes effort but is well worth it. Here are some tips for targeting individual analysts who can deliver significant ROI with their insights into what users are buying and why.

- **Their research rarely if ever lauds a vendor; instead it discusses new concepts from users.** This is a quick way to figure out where an analyst is coming from and if they are really dialed in to what's happening with users—their research will focus more on new theoretical concepts and frameworks for organizing what users think. There's more of a focus on business processes and their payoff rather than vendor coverage.

- **Analysts have visited more users onsite by a 3:1 margin versus vendors.** This is research in its purest and most powerful form. Being in touch, personally, with the users of technology is much more powerful than visiting with vendors. Sure, these kinds of analysts need to get the latest from vendors on what's new on the market so they can recommend technologies to users, but it's not the core focus. Being conversant enough with the users of technology to translate those needs not only for vendor's benefit but for other users at the same or comparable decision points is the main point.

- **They are speakers at conferences sponsored by industry organizations.** It's a big win for any analyst to be asked to speak at an industry's annual meeting—it's validation that their research is relevant to users. Look for user-centered at these events.

Lessons Learned

This chapter is meant to give you a start at getting a strategy together for generating strong ROI from the analyst firms you work with. Using a scorecard gives you the chance to level-set expectations with the analyst and advisory firms you work with and really manage the relationships to results. Many vendors are looking at analyst and advisory firms as discretionary expenses and a few CEOs have even said that they won't renew unless there is a very clear ROI from the expense. Keep these points in mind when getting a scorecard together and starting assessing ROI:

- **User references are the currency vendors trade with.** If you don't have a program for managing user references, get one now. You need to turn these customers into references for analysts because that's the only differentiator that many analyst firms look for. Try building a scorecard where your customers rank you to get a sense of how close or far away you are from the ability to generate references. If you don't have any references right now it's time to get out and see some customers soon and see if you can convert your most enthusiastic customers.

- **Do win/loss analysis on your own pipeline.** For any marketing department, this is critical to find new ways to serve the sales force. If the analyst firms you are working with have any impact at all on your potential prospects, win/loss analysis will bring that out.

- **Don't give up doing white papers on your own; you are losing valuable knowledge.** Instead of paying to get white papers done, grow this capability in your company. Use analyst firms to review them—that way you generate your own subject matter experts. And in complex areas like lean manufacturing strategies or product lifecycle management in consumer products goods, growing your own experts can be a very powerful strategy.

- **Webinars are the purest form of lead generation in analyst relations.** If your company's management is just obsessed with getting sales leads from analyst relations, then use webinars for new product introductions and major product announcements. Attendance varies by subject area and the analyst(s) you get to do the event, but it is common for leads from webinars eventually to turn into sales.

7

Handling Analyst Speaking Engagements

Day-in-the-Life: Judge Analysts By Their Research First

In the rush to get their user conference pulled together one software company made a last-minute call to one of their analyst firms to see if a very well-known analyst could make it for the keynote on a Monday night. It was six weeks until the conference when the call came from the vendor to the analyst firm. No problem, came the word back, they could send the VP asked for, and the price was $15,000 for the 1 hour presentation, plus travel and expenses. The software vendor agreed, paperwork was e-mailed and within an hour the deal was done and everyone started looking forward to the keynote, which such a seasoned industry veteran giving the presentation.

As part of the approval process to get the speaker, the CEO had to have a conversation—just to make sure the views of the market were consistent—and they were. So the task was quickly handed off to the PR Director and Analyst Relations people to run with. As everyone in product management, sales management, public relations, analyst relations and product marketing scrambled to get the event together no one really asked to see any preview slides.

A week before the event the Marketing VP panicked and realized that no one had ever reviewed the slides—and that the event was going to start the following Sunday. Making the panic even worse was the fact that the analyst was on the road for the next seven days leading up to the event—there was no chance to review slides before the event. Given the event being in Miami a thunderstorm anywhere in the eastern United States could completely disrupt travel schedules and leave just hours to review the slides just made the Marketing VP's anxiety worse. As the

Marketing VP boarded his flight to Miami later that day he couldn't stop thinking about that aspect of the conference—a huge unknown as this VP had never seen the analyst speak.

Finally the Marketing VP couldn't take the anxiety anymore and called the research firm, asking if he could get the cell phone of the analyst, stating he was concerned about the slides and he had not seen them yet. To be fair, the analyst should have sent a set, yet the conversation with the CEO had been so jovial and light-hearted no one seemed to think of that point. No one at the analyst firm had the analysts' cell phone but they did say they would e-mail him and ask for the slides. The customer service manager responsible for this account promptly fired off an urgent e-mail to the analyst asking for the slides—and no response—the analyst was presenting at a conference in India and connecting to get e-mail in hotels there was a hit-or-miss proposition.

With anxiety riding very high the Marketing VP fired off an e-mail asking for—really demanding—immediate response. Still nothing. Sunday night rolled around, the analyst got in late because of a thunderstorm—around 2am—and had a note to call the Marketing VP at any time. So at 2am he called the Marketing VP, who was awake working on his slides. After a really contentious few minutes the analyst offered to meet the VP in the lobby and show the slides right then and there. So they met, went over the slides—and the content was exactly out of the last major report and was right on target for the market direction.

I don't mean to be pedantic about this example but this happens much more than any software vendor or analyst firm would care to admit. What could have alleviated this Marketing VP getting totally stressed out? And by the way this is a tame example compared to what has happened when people's emotions get ahead of themselves. By the way this story really did happen and the interchanges at the hotel on the phone were pretty strained. Consider these take-aways if you are going to have an analyst speak at an event of yours:

- **Ask upfront for the slides to have time for at least two review cycles.** Personally I have done up to four or five edit cycles with enterprise software vendors on a slide deck I was to present at their Partner Conference on the West Coast. After the fifth iteration I really had empathy for the company's leaders and what they were trying to communicate. I could speak to their passions for their business through the slides, and it was a much more enjoyable experience for everyone. But this worked because the enterprise software vendor was all over the coordination of slide content and planned review time into their schedules, we both felt a lot more comfortable with the result.

- **When all else fails read what the analyst has done in the last year and have faith.** This is the single best strategy if you find yourself in the position of the Marketing VP in this example. Get a sense of where he analyst sees the industry going, what the current users are telling the analyst, and definitely go to your competitor's websites to listen to this analyst's previous webinars and presentations.

Best and Worst Practices

It's troubling how many vendors really want a marquee name at their events yet have no trust in the analyst, VP, or even research CEO to deliver unless they are micro-managed. If you are looking at having a big-name analyst in regardless of their title, get to know them first—don't just jump right into it. Clearly worst practices in managing speaking engagements is to just panic, spreading anxiety throughout your company and spilling into the analyst firm, only having to try and buy back your credibility by showering the analyst with gifts they will most likely not have room to take back with them anyway.

The following two sections detail both best and worst practices when working with analysts you hire for special events.

Best Practices In Managing Analysts At Events

1. **Build one month into your schedule to review content, messaging, your goals and the audience with the analyst you want to speak.** The actual time used during this month of review is just maybe 5–10 hours max, but given your and the analysts' travel schedules it may take a month of elapsed time to get the review cycles in.

2. **If the analyst is local meet in person for these review sessions.** Let's face it, you are in effect hiring the analyst as a part of your event and will reflect directly on your judgment and ability to execute the event. So go and meet whoever you're hiring—even take them to lunch.

3. **Get the analyst to buy into your perception of the market.** You can't buy this, but you can ask for feedback on whether the product strategies make sense given their view of the market. Not that the analysts have to be gatekeepers for the messaging at the event—that's your call—but by

taking time to prep them they have a chance to meld your messages with their view of the market.

4. **Don't overwhelm analysts with huge suites, deluxe accommodations or penthouses at the event.** This really looks bad if any other member of the conference sees the person(s) you are hiring to speak duck into the exclusive area of the resort—you could lose credibility and so could they by even connoting special treatment for their views. Stay away from showering them with these deluxe accommodations.

5. **Have the analyst there for the first sessions and introduce them at the start of the event.** You're paying to have your analyst of choice there, you want to make sure there is a sense of continuity to them being at the event and being involved. This is critical, even if the analyst balks.

6. **Send a thank-you note to the analyst and carbon copy the head of their business unit, and if it is a small company, send the note to the CEO.** This means so much more than a fifty pound gift basket that someone has to lug back on the plane. If the analyst just excelled way above and beyond your expectations invite them back again.

7. **If the speaking engagement is also a webinar, be sure to get the speaker phone and webinar software running two or more times beforehand.** When it's a combined event don't assume that since the speaker(s) are there that the technology is. Be sure to run through both the dial-up lines and the web presentations to make sure they are viewable outside your company, and that builds work; in short, run through the entire event as if you were actually doing it, twice.

Worst Practices In Managing Analysts At Events

The biggest problems vendors have with events center on how time is managed with analysts beforehand and worst practices that make for uncomfortable situations during and after the event.

1. **Committing analysts to a strategy session with a client of yours without checking it out first.** Don't start committing the analyst's time at the event. One situation like this happened and the analyst had to leave immediately after their speech and the vendor had to apologize to their key prospects over not delivering a strategy session committed to.

2. **Skip the $500 personal electronics gadgets, DVD players and wireless PDAs as thank-you notes**. In an era of analyst interactions being scrutinized for lack of ethics, giving away expensive gifts, even in private, looks like a bribe. So don't do it. Give the analyst some time on their own—a rare commodity for the most traveled and in-demand analysts—and let them have a morning free. That is more valuable to them than any PDA with wireless access or some new personal DVD player. One analyst I know of donates these gifts to a local charity—he doesn't feel right having them around his office or home.

3. **No special travel arrangements or hotel accommodations**. You really don't want to be the poster child for the next article series in the software or hardware industry about lack of analyst ethics—and the bigger of a company you are and the greater the ability to afford these perks—the greater the risk of looking like there is a lack of ethics. Just play it like they are one of the rank-and-file of your company and stay away from any appearance of favoritism.

4. **Don't demand publicly that the analyst write about all the great insights from your event.** Some vendors are always angling for a mention in an article or report and the worst thing you can do at an event is try to embarrass an analyst into mentioning you. While analyst relations professionals refute this never happens, it does—and it is a very uncomfortable place to be.

Lessons Learned

Speaking engagements and webinars can be the most stressful part of working with an analyst firm. This chapter gives the lessons that companies have learned through experience. There's more than enough opportunity for confusion and missed assignments—in short, mixed expectations—with speaking engagements. Having gone through years of doing these, the best advice I can give you is to get know the analysts personally if at all possible. Do at least one planning meeting in person—even if it is combined with a visit to their offices for a briefing. Those face-to-face meetings I had in getting prepared for speaking engagements were the most effective; I was able to see first-hand what was critical in messaging to the vendors and provided I agreed with them, tailor my presentation to match what they wanted. That face-time is critical and must be pursued if at all possible.

Let's just summarize this point: you communicate better with people you trust, and that goes both ways. Meeting in person is the way to go.

Here are additional lessons learned from this chapter:

1. **Build a month's review cycle for slides.** Don't procrastinate and think with two weeks before the webinar there is time to get slides reviewed. With the travel schedules of analysts you want speaking for your company, a month can go by like a week.

2. **Reward analysts with open time and not lavish gifts.** Open time to analysts is more valuable than a personal DVD player, TV, iPOD, or huge gift basket. Time to catch up on reports, time to just relax and golf—that is what analysts appreciate. Stay away from the high ticket gifts because you also don't want to appear to be unethical and trying to swerve their judgments. One prominent analyst who is a VP in a research firm donates the many iPAQs and personal DVD players he receives every year. That's class.

3. **Don't commit analysts days for them without checking first.** There are firms that think that since they have hired an analyst for a speaking engagement they have them for the full time of the event and commit them to meetings. If you want this level of service be honest and let the analyst firm know that. No one likes big surprises like that.

4. **Over-communicate the agenda and the structure of the meeting.** As the agenda progresses you need to have the analyst firm's contacts you have stay in touch with its progress.

8

Managing Analyst Transitions

Day-in-the-Life: Should you recruit an analyst when they are let go?

You've invested several years in a relationship with an analyst to the point where they know not only your company's strengths, weaknesses, opportunities, threats and even potential acquisitions. You've built product strategies, sales and service programs, and even architected your competitive analysis strategies from their input. Sometimes analysts become part of the core team of your company mainly due to their ability to deliver significant value in a short period of time.

With pressure on analyst organizations to concentrate on the areas of coverage that can deliver the greatest revenue, the decision is made to discontinue analysts in your market arena. The analyst who is so valuable to your company is now a free agent. Depending on the level of experience the analysts have that become free agents, some become full-time consultants, and others choose to go into a separate industry. Still others jump right back into research with another firm.

As research and advisory firms consolidate and more analysts are let go, there's going to be more of an opportunity to hire these industry experts. The world's leading software companies are capitalizing on industry experts in search of work. Increasing their staffs in vertical market organizations, pre-sales and sales support, product leadership, analyst relations and even executive management these larger vendors want product strategy more than evangelism.

Deciding if this strategy of recruiting analysts for you starts with the following considerations:

- **Do the analysts you work with have the ability to contribute while they learn your culture?** The best hires out of the analyst community can quickly start contributing—they can traverse from the strategic to the tactical in discussions and action items. If all you want is an analyst to fill a tactical role be sure to give the expectation very clearly—as analysts get pulled in both strategic and tactical directions—and many of them excel at one and struggle at the other. Look at the potential hiring of an analyst through this lens first.

- **How does the work ethic in your company matches the analyst firms'?** There is a big difference between some vendor's environments and the environments within analyst firms. In the world of analysts there are those small firms where every analyst needs to publish research often, and then there are the larger, more slow-moving analyst firms where publishing is not as important as bringing in new clients. Some analysts are not expected to publish for months—now in the world of the smaller research firm that is like a vacation! So just be aware of what level of work was required as an analyst compared to what you're going to need.

- **Travel requirements: pro and con.** Typically the longer someone has been an analyst the longer they have been on the road, sometimes 50% of the time. What I've seen is that analysts want to be on the road *more* or they want to completely cut back. For some analysts being on the road gives them a sense of being more involved in their clients' work—so just gauge this expectation during an initial discussion and see where the analyst is you want to hire.

- **Really believe in your company or just taking a new job?** This is tough to gauge but before you hire an analyst who covered your market space and company but have a candid, honest discussion before you bring someone from the research community onboard. Ask for and get a critical assessment of the company for their perspective and what they would most want to change. You have to find out if the person you're hiring is just looking for an interim job or if they really want to bring passion to their job and change the company for the better. Again, tough to get to but it is a must-have as people inside will have high expectations already from someone like an analyst coming onboard.

The Ethics of an Analyst Joining a Vendor Client

When analysts prove their ability to anticipate the direction of a market and influence technology users at the same time, vendors quietly begin recruiting them. What's important to realize is that the analysts tracking your industry, company or even to the product line level are approached to join vendors more often than any of them would openly admit to. Recruiting is happening all the time between vendors and analysts. The ethics of an analyst are often on the line regarding how they handle it. Here are some situations to be concerned about when an analyst leaves for a competing vendor:

- **Evangelists.** Vendors also hire analysts to hit the road and give presentations on their company's virtues and future plans. For many analysts this is a good exit path from research organizations, and gives many of them the chance to continue working with vendor clients and their customers.

- **Fueling Product Management.** Analysts are often seen as a natural fit with product management teams in many companies, this is the organization that interacts with and gets the most guidance from research companies.

- **Marketing and Competitive Analysis Champions.** Leading enterprise software vendors hire analysts to gain their insights into user requirements, competitive analysis and for assistance with getting their messaging and positioning out to the industry. The fact that analysts are often very well known in their market arenas is a drawing card for these larger companies, and it's common to see seminars and webinar series built around the most senior of analysts after being recruited by larger vendors.

- **Vendors are buying sales pipelines.** Analysts who have a major impact on companies acquiring technology are often recruited for the sales deals they carry in their head. Vendors like to go after "money analysts" that have proven their ability to influence sales. While no one will ever talk about these kinds of recruiting arrangements they do happen. What's ironic about these situations is that the analyst has many times short-listed companies that most closely align with the needs of acquiring companies. If the vendor trying to recruit the analyst wasn't short-listed to begin with, getting in on deals puts the analyst's credibility on the line. In each arena of the market there are examples of these recruiting practices, with many of them ending just as quickly as they began.

  - **Take-aways:**

    - Protect all deals you are in that were generated from analyst recommendations with NDAs that extend past the analyst's employment with the research organization.

    - Track how many deals your analyst organizations bring you and be sure to capture the specifics behind how you were able to win the sale.

- This is not ethical in the least and analysts who do sell out the pipelines they are aware of bear the brunt of the loss of credibility. Every once in a while analysts will get caught in this, yet the majority of those spoken with run from these situations.

APPENDIX

Industry Analyst Firms

Aberdeen
One Boston Place
Boston, MA 02108
USA
TEL: 1 617 723 7890
FAX: 1 617 723 7897
www aberdeen com

Access Markets International
546 Fifth Avenue, 22nd Floor
New York, NY 10036
USA
TEL: 1 212 944 5100
FAX: 1 212 944 2288
www ami-usa com
jrezac@ami-partners com

Advanced Tech Monitor
500 West Cummings Park, Suite 5200
Woburn, MA 01801
USA
Tel: 1 781 939 2500/1 800 767 9499
Fax: 1 781 939 2577
www advancetechmonitor com
cs@advancetechmonitor com

Advanced Media Strategies
PO Box 1991
Issaquah, WA 98027

USA
www tvstrategies com
info@tvstrategies com

AMR Research
125 Summer Street
Boston, MA 02110-1616
Tel: 617-542-6600
Fax: 617-542-5670
www amrresearch com
info@amrresearch com

Arlen Communications
7315 Wisconsin Avenue, Suite 600E
Bethesda, MD 20814
USA
TEL: 1 301 656 7940
FAX: 1 301 656 3204
www arlencommunications com
gary@arlencom com

ARS Inc,
8008 Girard Ave, Suite #145
La Jolla, CA 92037
USA
TEL: 1 858 551 0008
FAX: 1 858 551 0009
www ars1 com
sales@ars1 com

Boston Consulting Group
Exchange Place, 31st Floor
Boston, MA 02109
USA
TEL: 1 617 973 1200
FAX: 1 617 973 1339
www bcg com

Business Intelligence
22-24 Worple Road
Wimbledon
London SW19 4DD
UK
TEL: 44 (0)208 879 3300
www business-intelligence co uk
jane mills@business-intelligence co uk

BWE Research
2844 E Michelle Way, Ste 1101
Gilbert, AZ 85234
USA
TEL: 1 480 218 4441
FAX: 1 480 218 4442
www bbwexchange com
rhoskins@bbwexchange com

Cahners In-Stat Group
6909 East Greenway Parkway, Suite 250
Scottsdale, AZ 85254
USA
TEL: 1 480 483 4440
FAX: 1 480 483 0400
www instat com
info@instat com

Canalysis com
100 Longwater Avenue,
Green Park
Reading, Berks, RG2 6GP
UK
TEL: 44 118 945 0173
FAX: 44 118 945 0186
www canalys com
info@canalys com

CAP Ventures
600 Cordwainer Drive

Norwell, MA 02061
USA
TEL: 1 781 871 9000
FAX: 1 781 871 3861
www capv com
info@capv com

Celent Communications
183 State Street, 5th Floor
Boston, Massachusetts 02109
USA
TEL: 1 617 573 9450
FAX: 1 617 573 9455
www celent com
info@celent com

The Chandler Group
The Sanctuary Tower, Suite 210
4400 North Federal Highway
Boca Raton, FL
USA
1 561 392 9220
1 561 272 2668
www thechandlergroup com
info@chandler com

CIMData
3909 Research Park Drive
Ann Arbor, MI 48108
USA
TEL: 1 734 668 9922
FAX: 1 734 668 1957
www cimdata com
info@CIMdata com

Clipper Group
888 Worcester Street, Suite 90
Worcester, MA 02482
USA

TEL: 1 781 235 0085
FAX: 1 781 235 5454
www clipper com
info@clipper com

Computer Industry Researchers
P O Box 5387
Charlottesville, VA 22905
USA
TEL: 1 804 984 0245
FAX: 1 804 984 0247
www cir-inc com
info@cir-inc com

Cutter Consortium
37 Broadway, Suite 1
Arlington, MA 02474
USA
TEL: 1 781 641 5118/800 964 5118
FAX: 1 781 648 1950/800 888 1816
www cutter com
service@cutter com

EDVenture Holdings
104 Fifth Avenue, 20th floor
New York, NY 10011
USA
TEL: 1 212 924 8800
FAX: 1 212 924 0240
www edventure com
us@edventure com

Enterprise Storage Group
189 West Street
Milford, MA 01757
USA
TEL: 1 508 482 0188
FAX: 1 508 482 0128

www enterprisestoragegroup com
info@enterprisestoragegroup com

EuroLAN Research
Technology Transfer Centre, Silwood Park
Ascot, Berkshire, SL5 7PW
UK
TEL: 44 (0)1344 291080
FAX: 44 (0)1344 872230
www eurolanresearch com
info@eurolanresearch com

Faulkner Information Services
114 Cooper Center
7905 Browning Road
Pennsauken, NJ 08109-4319
USA
TEL: 1 856 662 2070/800 843 0460
www faulkner com
faulkner@faulkner com

Forrester Research
400 Technology Square
Cambridge, MA 02139
USA
TEL: 1 617 497 7090
FAX: 1 617 613 5000
www forrester com

Freeman Reports
12010 MacDonald Drive
Ojai, CA 93023-9714
USA
TEL: 1 805 649 5135
FAX: 1 805 649 5136
www freemanreports com
bob@freemanreports com

Frost & Sullivan
1040 East Brokaw Road
San Jose, CA 95131-2309
USA
TEL: 1 877 463 7678
FAX: 1 888 690 3329
www frost com

Fuld and Company
126 Charles Street
Cambridge, MA 02141
USA
TEL: 1 617 492 5900
FAX: 1 617 492 7108
www fuld com
info@fuld com

Gartner Dataquest
600 Delran Parkway
Delran, NJ 08075
USA
TEL: 1 856 764 0100/800 328 2776
FAX: 1 856 764 2814
www gartner com
info@gartner com

Gartner
56 Top Gallant Road P O Box 10212
Stamford, CT 06904-2212
USA
TEL: 1 203 316 1111
FAX: 1 203 316 6300
www gartner com
gginfo@gartner com

IDC
5 Speen Street
Framingham, MA 01701
USA

TEL: 1 508 872 8200
FAX: n/a
www idc com

Jon Peddie Research
4 Saint Gabrielle Court
Tiburon, CA 94920-1619
USA
TEL: 1 415 435 9368
FAX:
www jonpeddie com
jon@jonpeddie com

Juniper Research
Worting House
Worting Business Park
Basingstoke, Hampshire
RG23 8PY
UK
TEL: 44 (0)1256 345612
FAX:
www juniperresearch com
info@juniperresearch com

Jupiter Research
21 Astor Place
New York, NY 10003
USA
TEL: 1 212 780 6060
FAX: 1 212 780 6075
www jupiterresearch com
jupiter@jmm com

Nucleus Research
36 Washington Street
Wellesley MA 02481
USA
TEL: 1 781 416 2900
FAX: 1 781 416 5252

www nucleusresearch com
info@NucleusResearch com

Ovum
Cardinal Tower
12 Farringdon Road
London EC1M 3HS
UK
TEL: 44 (0)207 551 9000
FAX: 44 (0)207 551 9090
www ovum com
webinfo@ovum com

Ovum Holway
2 St Georges Yard
Farnham, Surrey GU7 7LW
UK
TEL: 44 (0)1252 740900
FAX: 44 (0)1252 740919
www ovumholway com
mail@ovumholway com

Patricia Seybold Group
210 Commercial Street
Boston, MA 02109
USA
TEL: 1 617 742 5200
FAX: 1 617 742 1028
www psgroup com
feedback@psgroup com

Sage Research
220 North Main Street, Suite 102
Natick, MA 01760
USA
TEL: 1 508 655 5400
FAX: 1 508 655 5516
www sageresearch com
info@sageresearch com

The451
137 5th Ave, 12th floor
New York, NY 10010
USA
TEL: 1 212 505 3030
FAX: 1 212 505 2630
www the451 com
nyeditorial@the451 com

Venture Development Corporation
One Apple Hill Drive, P O B 8190
Suite 206
Natick, MA 01760
USA
TEL: 1 508-653-9000
FAX: 1 508-653-9836
www vdc-corp com
info@vdc-corp com

Wohl Associates
915 Montgomery Avenue, Suite 309
Narberth, PA 19072
USA
TEL: 1 610 667 4842
FAX: 1 610 667 3081
www wohl com
opinions@wohl com

Yankee Group
31 St James Avenue
Boston, MA 02116-4114
USA
TEL: 1 617 956 5000
FAX: 1 617 956 5005
www yankeegroup com

0-595-33462-8

Printed in the United States
52728LVS00003BA/206